SCHOLASTIC Phonics

Rescue Dogs

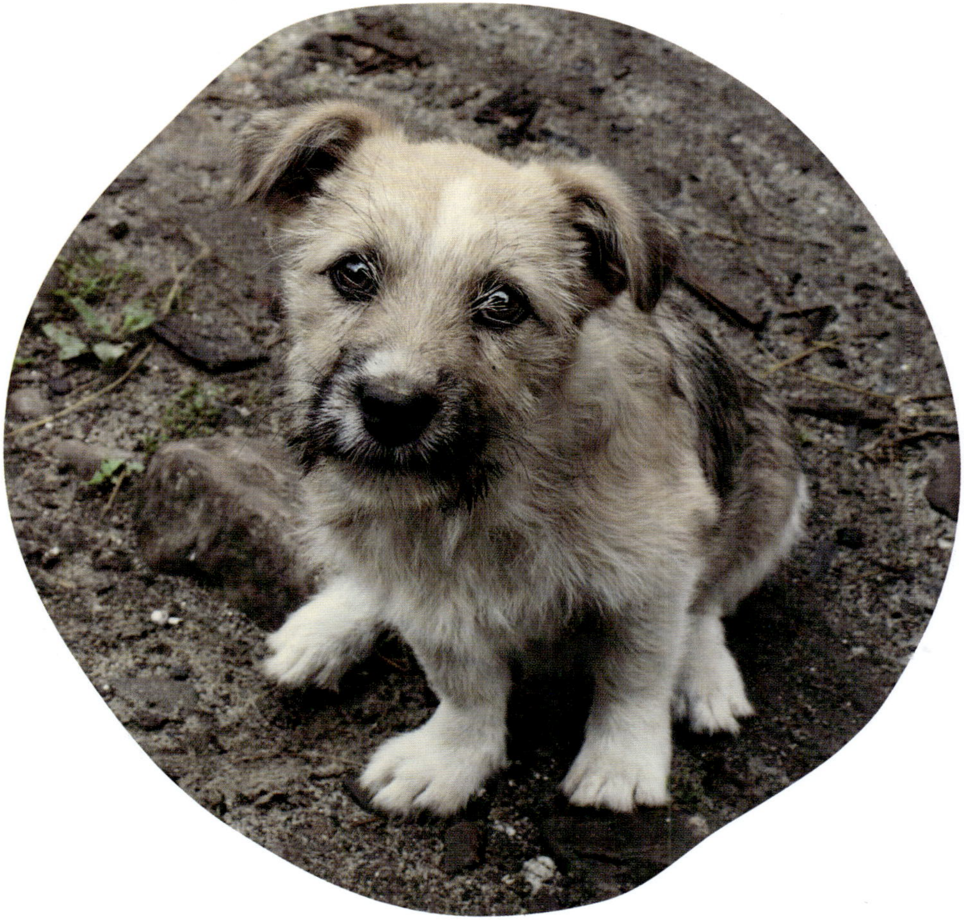

Published in the UK by Scholastic Education, 2023
Scholastic Distribution Centre, Bosworth Avenue, Tournament Fields, Warwick, CV34 6UQ
Scholastic Ireland, 89E Lagan Road, Dublin Industrial Estate, Glasnevin, Dublin, D11 HP5F

SCHOLASTIC and associated logos are trademarks and/or registered trademarks of Scholastic Inc.
www.scholastic.co.uk
© 2023 Scholastic
123456789 3456789012

Printed by Ashford Colour Press
The book is made of materials from well-managed, FSC®-certified forests and other controlled sources.

A CIP catalogue record for this book is available from the British Library.
ISBN 978-0702-32103-0

All rights reserved. This book is sold subject to the condition that it shall not, by way of trade or otherwise, be lent, hired out or otherwise circulated in any form of binding or cover other than that in which it is published. No part of this publication may be reproduced, stored in a retrieval system, or transmitted in any form or by any other means (electronic, mechanical, photocopying, recording or otherwise) without prior written permission of Scholastic.

Every effort has been made to trace copyright holders for the works reproduced in this publication, and the publishers apologise for any inadvertent omissions.

Author
Rachel Russ

Editorial team
Rachel Morgan, Vicki Yates, Alison Gilbert, Jennie Clifford

Design team
Dipa Mistry, Andrea Lewis, We Are Grace

Photographs
Cover David Baileys/iStock
p1, 4 Irina Baturina/Shutterstock
p5, 18, 19, 24 mladenbalinovac/iStock
p6-7, 24 PavelKant/Shutterstock
p8 kali9/iStock
p3, 9 andresr/iStock
p10-11 Gea Veenstra/iStock
p12, 20-21, 24 PeopleImages.com - Yuri A/Shutterstock
p13 alexei_tm/iStock
p14 Olena Yakobchuk/Shutterstock
p15 jeffbergen/iStock
p16-17 StefaNikolic/iStock
p22-23 hedgehog94/Shutterstock

Help your child to read!

This book practises these letters and letter sounds.
Point and say the sounds with your child:

- ay (as in 'may')
- ou (as in 'about')
- oy (as in 'boy')
- ea (as in 'each')
- ue (as in 'rescue')
- u (as in 'music')

Your child may need help to read these common tricky words:

all, of, be, no, are, the, when, to, by, some, they, have, put, someone, today, you

Before reading
- Look at the cover picture and read the title together. Read the back cover blurb to your child.
- Ask your child: *Do you have a pet? What is it like?*
- Talk about the image in the magnifying glass.

During reading
- If your child gets stuck on a word, remind them to sound it out and then blend the sounds to read the word: r-e-s-c-ue, rescue.
- If they are still stuck, show them how to read the word.
- Enjoy looking at the pictures together. Pause to talk about the information.

After reading
- Talk about the images on page 24. What can your child tell you about them?
- Ask your child: *What is the first thing that happens to a dog when it is taken to a shelter?*
- Discuss which page your child found most interesting or surprising.

Dog shelters rescue dogs in need.

All sorts of dogs can be found in a shelter.

Dogs end up at shelters for lots of reasons. It may be that a person can no longer keep a dog.

Stray dogs are found on the street and rescued.

When it first gets to the shelter, a dog is checked by a vet. Is it a boy or a girl? Is it ill or hurt?

The vet treats the dog if it is ill.

Some dogs are frightened due to the smells and sounds in a shelter. Dogs may be frightened of humans.

Music can be soothing for stressed dogs.

Helpers at the shelter clean and feed the dogs.

They let the dogs have a run around. Some dogs enjoy playing with toys too.

A record about each dog is put on to the computer.

It might be found by someone looking on the internet for a dog to adopt.

Helpers must select the right person to meet each dog's needs.

Blue is waiting for someone to adopt him.

Helpers continue to feed and play with each dog until it's adopted.

Today, Troy has been adopted. The helpers have found the perfect setting for him.

If you get a pet, you may wish to have a look at a rescue shelter.

Talk about it!